The Duke Basketball Trivia Challenge

Steve Biddison

Copyright © 2018 Steve Biddison
Duke Basketball Digest
All rights reserved.

ISBN-13:
978-1717099020

ISBN-10:
1717099025

DEDICATION

This book is dedicated to Duke basketball fans:

First to my son, Landry, who followed in his father's footsteps in becoming a Duke basketball fan.

To my brother, Mark, who has been a Duke basketball fan almost as long as I have.

To my nephew, Micah, we followed in his father's and uncle's footsteps in becoming a Duke basketball fan.

To my best friend in coaching, Bill Avey. What a pleasant surprise to find that we both had a love for Duke basketball.

To Coach Mike Krzyzewski, my inspiration as a coach and the reason I became a Duke fan.

And of course, the Cameron Crazies (how I loved standing with you when I attended a game) and all Duke fans.

All Pictures in this book were taken by Steve Biddison on one of his trips to Duke University.

CONTENTS

	Introduction	i
1	Duke All-Time Greats	1
2	My Personal All-Time Lists of Duke Players	8
3	By the Numbers	12
4	By the Names	18
5	Coach K	23
6	Duke University and Cameron Indoor Stadium	27
7	ACC Rivals and Other Famous Games	31
8	The NCAA Tournament	36
9	Duke in the NBA	49
10	Duke Trivia Challenge Answers	52

INTRODUCTION

I hope you enjoy this Duke Basketball Trivia Challenge. This is not only your chance to see how much you know about your favorite college basketball program, but it is also your opportunity to name your own all-time favorite lists of Duke players.

This Duke Basketball Trivia Challenge book promises to take you back through the years of watching Duke basketball and bring back some of the great memories you experienced as a Duke fan. You will recall players, games, and opponents as you seek to answer as many questions as you can.

I have taken great efforts to try to ensure that as of the end of the 2018 college basketball season, all the answers in the answer in the answer section are correct. However, in the event that my answer is either wrong or incomplete, I apologize and when I make another edition, I will fix the problem.

On the questions that have you form your personal opinions or lists, I give you my lists in the answer section. My list is only my opinion and is not considered to be the "correct" answer. You are free to differ in your opinion.

You could research each question and probably find the answers on the internet. However, I believe it will be more fun for you to see how much you know already before researching. Use your research (or the answer section) to fill in the blanks.

Enjoy your time in the book and as always *Go Duke*

DUKE ALL-TIME GREATS

The Duke Blue Devils have had many great and memorable players come through their program over the years. In this section, you will be tested on your Blue Devil player knowledge. For each question that asks for a listing, list as many of these players as you can from memory. You can always go back and research it to fill in the blanks. But what fun is that?

Jersey Retirements

1. As of 2018, there have been 13 jerseys that hang in the rafters of Cameron. List the Players and Their Numbers Who have had their jerseys retired.

    1)

    2)

    3)

    4)

5)

6)

7)

8)

9)

10)

11)

12)

13)

Player of the Year Awards

There have been many Duke players who have received various player of the year awards. See how many you can name without looking them up. Hints are sometimes provided

2. As of 2018, there have been six different Duke players named National Defensive Player of the Year. Who were they?

1)

2)

3)

4)

5)

6)

3. Which Duke player was named National Defensive Player of the year in three different seasons?

4. As of 2018, there have been 9 Duke players name National Player of the Year. Can you name them?

1)

2)

3)

4)

5)

6)

7)

8)

9)

5. Name the only two Duke players who have won National Player of the Year in two different seasons

1)

2)

6. As of 2018, there have been 3 Duke freshmen who have won the National Freshman of the Year Award. Who are they?

1)

2)

3)

7. As of 2018, there have been 14 Duke players named ACC Player of the Year. Without looking it up, how many can you name?

1)

2)

3)

4)

5)

6)

7)

8)

9)

10)

11)

12)

13)

14)

8. Which two players have won ACC player of the year in two different years?

1)

2)

9. As of 2018, there have been 10 Duke freshmen that have been named ACC Freshman of the Year. How many can you name without looking it up?

1)

2)

3)

4)

5)

6)

7)

8)

9)

10)

10. As of 2018, there have only been two players in ACC history who have been named both ACC Freshman of the Year and ACC Player of the Year in the same season. Who were they?

1)

2)

Duke Records

There are so many great basketball players that have come through Duke University that it is almost impossible to remember even a small percentage of them. However, some have stood about above the rest and have etched their name in the school record books. Let's see how many of those record holders you can name from memory

11. Who is Duke's career leader in number of games played?

12. Who is Duke's career leader in minutes played?

13. Who holds the freshman scoring record at Duke?

14. Who holds the freshman rebounding record at Duke?

15. Who is Duke's all-time scoring leader?

16. Who is Duke's all-time assist leader?

17. Who is Duke's all-time leader in rebounds?

18. Who is Duke's all-time leader in steals?

19. Who is Duke's all-time leader in blocks?

20. Who is Duke's all-time leader in Free throw percentage?

21. Who is Duke's all-time leader in 3 point percentage (minimums 70 attempts)?

22. Who is Duke all-time leader in field goal percentage?

23. Who is Duke's all-time leader in charges taken?

24. Who has the most dunks in Duke history?

25. Which two players share the Duke record for most three point shots made in a game?

    1)

    2)

26. Which two players share the record for the most blocked shots in a single game? How many did they each block?

    1)

    2)

27. Who holds the Duke record for most assists in a game? How many assists did he have?

MY PERSONAL ALL-TIME LISTS OF GREAT DUKE PLAYERS

This chapter is your chance to make your All-Time Duke teams. In some cases, the questions might come from times before you were a Duke basketball fan. That's okay. Other questions will test your Duke memory for as far back as you can go. Have fun! Enjoy putting together your own favorite Duke teams.

28. If you could add a jersey (or two) to hang from the rafters of Cameron, who would you add and why?

29. What Duke players or coaches have you personally met?

30. Who is your number one all-time favorite Duke player and why?

Name your personal All-Time List of Duke Players

    31. **First Team**

        PG

        Wing

        Wing

        Post

        Post

    32. **Second Team**

        PG

        Wing

        Wing

        Post

        Post

    33. **Third Team**

        PG

        Wing

        Wing

Post

Post

34. Who is your All-Time Freshman team (does not have to be a one and done player, but can be)?

PG

Wing

Wing

Post

Post

Other

Other

35. Who is your All-Time 4 year player team?

PG

Wing

Wing

Post

Post

Other

Other

Your All Decade Teams

36. 1970's

      PG

      Wing

      Wing

      Post

      Post

      Other

      Other

37. 1980's

      PG

      Wing

      Wing

      Post

      Post

      Other

      Other

38. 1990's

    PG

    Wing

    Wing

    Post

    Post

    Other

    Other

39. 2000-2009

    PG

    Wing

    Wing

    Post

    Post

    Other

    Other

40. 2010-2019

    PG

    Wing

    Wing

    Post

    Post

    Other

    Other

BY THE NUMBERS

You have (hopefully) already been able to name all the jersey numbers that have been retired (though some may have been re-issued at one point). But there are a many other numbers that have been on uniforms of Duke players that have never hung from the rafters at Cameron. See how many you can name.

41. Name at least one player who has worn each number in a Duke uniform

#0

#1

#2

#3

#4

#5

#10

#11

#12

#13

#14

#15

#20

#21

#22

#23

#24

#25

#30

#31

#32

#33

#34

#35

#40

#41

#42

#43

#44

#45

#50

#51

#52

#53

#54

#55

Let's look at some significant numbers in Duke Basketball History.

42. What was the highest scoring average for any Duke team? How many points did they average?

43. What is the most number of wins in a season by a Duke team?

44. What is the most points one player scored in a single game in Duke history? Who did it and how many points did he score?

45. What year was a Coach K led Duke team first ranked in the top 10 in the Final AP Poll?

46. What year did Duke play its first basketball game?

BY THE NAMES

It's one thing to be remembered by a number, but it is something else to be remembered by your name. There have been hundreds upon hundreds of players come through the Duke program and they each had a name. Some of them had nicknames. Let's see how well we remember some of our Blue Devil hero names.

47. Here is a challenge for you. Out of the 26 letters in the alphabet, how many can you attach to the last name of a Duke basketball player? Every letter might not have a last name associated with it and in that case, you could use a first name. Choose your favorite Duke player by their letter in the alphabet.

A.

B.

C.

D.

E.

F.

G.

H.

I.

J.

K.

L.

M.

N.

O.

P.

Q.

R.

S.

T.

U.

V.

W.

X.

Y.

Z.

48. Which former Duke player became President Obama's personal trainer?

Nicknames

49. Who was *The Alaskan Assassin?*

50. What player did the Duke fans affectionately call *Chief?*

51. Who was *The Minister of Defense?*

52. Who was termed *The Landlord?*

53. Who was nicknamed *Tinkerbell?*

54. Who was known as the *Gman?*

Other Name Related Trivia

55. What was the original name of Duke University?

56. What Duke player had a father who was a former All-pro NFL running back?

57. What three brothers have won national championships at Duke?

58. What organization was the inspiration behind naming the mascot, *Blue Devils?*

59. Who actually decided to name the mascot the *Blue Devils?*

60. Who is Duke University named after?

61. *The One and Done Rule* officially began on in 2006, who was Duke's first official one and done player?

62. As of the end of the 2018 season, what Duke assistant coaches have won the NCAA National Championship both as a player and a coach?

63. In the history of Duke basketball, there have been 3 father/son combinations that played for Duke. Who are they?

64. What do the Duke players do to signify that they are going to make a stand on defense?

COACH K

He has been called the G.O.A.T – The Greatest of All Time. But before he was the greatest, he was a little-known coach with a name that no one could pronounce. Let's see just how much you know about the winningest coach in NCAA history.

65. Of what national decent did Coach K come from?

66. What did Coach K's father do for a living?

67. What kind of work did his mother do?

68. Coach K has always talked about his older brother being his hero. What did Bill Krzyzewski do for a living?

69. What did Coach K's friends call him when he was growing up?

70. What is Coach K's wife name?

71. How many daughters does Coach K have? Can you name them?

72. How many grandchildren does Coach K have?

73. Where did Coach K coach before taking the Duke job?

74. As a graduate assistant coach, who did Coach K coach under for a year?

75. What was Coach K's rank in the army?

76. How many wins did Coach K have prior to coming to Duke?

77. Who recommended Coach K to then Duke Athletic Director Tom Butters?

78. Who was Coach K's very first prize recruit?

79. What infamous loss early in his Duke tenure, prompted Coach K to say, "Here's to never forgetting."

80. How many times has Coach K won the National Coach of the Year Award? Can you name the years?

81. How many times has Coach K won the ACC Coach of the Year Award? Can you name the years?

82. Who was Duke playing when Coach K became the winningest coach in NCAA men's basketball history?

83. Where was Duke playing when Coach K became the winningest coach in NCAA men's basketball history?

84. Who was Duke playing when Coach K won his 1000th game?

85. Where was Duke playing when Coach K won his 1000th game?

86. Who was Duke playing when Coach K won his 1000th game as the coach at Duke?

87. Where was Duke playing when Coach won his 1000th game as the coach at Duke?

88. What is Coach K's overall international record in coaching TEAM USA?

89. Where is Coach K's office?

90. What iconic symbol of Coach K's basketball philosophy is engraved into the 2001 National Championship ring? It is also a sculpture in his office?

91. This symbol is also an acronym. What does it stand for?

92. Name the only college basketball teams that Coach K has a losing record against while at Duke

93. When was Coach K inducted into the Basketball Hall of Fame?

94. Who was the first number one ranked team that Coach K beat?

DUKE UNIVERSITY AND CAMERON INDOOR STADIUM

Every Duke fan should at least one time in their life take a pilgrimage to Duke University and Cameron Indoor Stadium. Nestled in the trees of North Carolina, it is a campus bristling with historical and gothic architecture. Even a facelift to Cameron Indoor Stadium does not detract from history of the place that some consider to be the mecca of college basketball.

Only at Duke University will you find not only the rich basketball history, but the crazy fans who are not only considered by some to be the best in college basketball, but they also have a unique way of determining who gets tickets to the big games. They camp in a place known as Krzyzewskiville

Let's see how much history you know about Duke University, but mainly about Cameron Indoor Stadium and the famed Krzyzewskiville site.

95. What are the Duke basketball fans called in their home games?

96. What two words do the fans chant at Cameron when the opposing player who just fouled out sits down?

97. Whose bust famously sits outside Cameron Indoor Stadium?

98. What year was Cameron Indoor Stadium built?

99. What is the current seating/standing capacity of Cameron?

100. What is the song sung during every game in Cameron that the crowd jumps up and down during the chorus? Fill in the blanks. "_____ we _____"

101. According to legend, what did Eddie Cameron and Wallace Wade use to sketch and design the basketball stadium?

102. What was the original name of Cameron Indoor Stadium?

103. What year was the stadium renamed Cameron Indoor Stadium?

104. Who was the opponent for the game when the stadium was officially renamed Cameron Indoor Stadium?

105. In what game did the now famous chant "air ball" originate?

106. How many different players recruited by Coach K and stayed four years never were part of a team that hung a banner in the rafters?

107. In what year was the basketball court inside Cameron Indoor Stadium officially named *Coach K Court*

108. How was the initial building of the stadium initially funded?

      a.   Gifts from boosters?
      b.   Duke football team's Rose Bowl earnings
      c.   Fund raisers by the athletic department
      d.   Money earned from Television royalties

109. What is the most consecutive number of victories at Cameron?

110. Three different years, Duke has won 17 games at Cameron. Which years did they accomplish this?

111. Describe where is Krzyzewskiville located?

112. How many can occupy a single tent in Krzyzewskiville?

113. What year did Krzyzewskiville begin?

114. How many total tents are allowed in Krzyzewskiville?

115. In a group is registered at *black registration* (the first wave), how many people must occupy a tent at any time during the day?

116. In a group is registered at *black registration* (the first wave), how many people must occupy a tent at night?

117. Just because you want to camp in Krzyzewskiville doesn't mean you automatically get to. How do they determine if you get in and where your tent is located?

118. Who is credited for the beginning of Krzyzewskiville?

ACC RIVALS AND OTHER FAMOUS GAMES

There is no other conference in college basketball that rivals the Atlantic Coast Conference. Year in and year out they have multiple ranked teams, often two to three teams ranked in the top 10 in the country. It seems to be unusual if there is not an ACC team playing in the Final Four.

Once upon a time, from top to bottom it was a conference that boasted incredible teams and talent. But over time, the ACC has changed and there are now (as of 2018) 15 teams in the conference. That has caused the rivalry between some of the programs to not be as great as it once was. It is still, however, a conference full of intense rivalries.

Let's see how much you know about the ACC.

119. Other than Durham, what city has Duke won the most games in?

120. Other than Coach K, list your personal five all-time favorite ACC coaches.

  1)

  2)

  3)

  4)

  5)

121. How many ACC schools does Duke NOT hold an all-time head to head advantage with? Name them?

122. What is Duke's won/loss record against UNC during the Coach K era?

123. What ACC team does Duke have the most all-time victories against?

124. Usually, in the last home game of the year, also known as Senior Night, Coach K likes to take his Seniors out of the game in the final minute so they can receive one last cheer from the home crowd. However, sometimes due to the closeness of the game, he doesn't have the opportunity to do that. In his final home game on Senior Night, as time expired in a two-point come from behind victory, which player made a beeline sprint straight to Coach K giving him a big hug? Hint: It is still often shown on ESPN highlights.

125. Besides Bobby Hurley, who is the number one assist man in ACC history, which other Blue Devil is ranked in the top 5 in the ACC in career assists?

126. Who holds the record for the most number of ACC wins in a career?

127. As of the tournament in 2018, how many ACC tournaments has Duke won?

128. What year was the ACC formed and who were the founding members?

    Year –

        1)

        2)

        3)

        4)

        5)

        6)

        7)

129. How far apart are the campuses of Duke and North Carolina?

130. What is the nickname given to "road" that runs from Duke to UNC to NC State?

131. In his final home game, what did Gene Banks throw into the crowd?

132. How many conferences does Duke have a losing record against?

133. Other than the ACC, which conference does Duke have the most number of wins against?

134. Duke holds the ACC record with the most consecutive ACC Tournament titles. How many years in a row did the win it?

135. Duke holds the ACC record for most consecutive ACC victories. What year(s) did they accomplish this and how long was the streak?

136. Duke holds the ACC record for most consecutive ACC **road** victories. What year(s) did they accomplish this and how long was the streak?

137. What was Duke's largest margin of victory ever?

138. What was the biggest halftime deficit that Duke has come back from to win and who was the opponent? (this is not an ACC game)

139. Who hit a buzzer beating three-point shot in 2012 to beat UNC?

140. What was the deficit in the final minute of the road game against Maryland before the comeback known as *The Miracle Minute* took place?

141. In 1979, Duke held UNC scoreless for the entire first half. What was the halftime score and what was the final score of the game?

142. As of 2018, only one ACC team had each of their five starters named to an All-ACC team? Which Duke team accomplish this? Name the five players.

    1)

    2)

    3)

    4)

    5)

THE NCAA TOURNAMENT

The best way to end any season for a Duke basketball fan is to watch our team cut down the nets before we are reminded of the great tournament run with the playing of *One Shining Moment*. As of 2018, we have seen the Blue Devils accept the National Championship Trophy 5 times.

Let's see how much you know about Duke's play in the NCAA Tournament and those National Championship Teams.

143. What year did a Coach K coached Duke receive its first NCAA Tournament bid?

144. What year did Duke first play in the Final Four?

145. There have been three players in NCAA history that have played in four Final Fours. Who were they?

1)

2)

3)

146. What was the largest deficit Duke had in the 2001 National Semi-final game against Maryland before coming back to win it?

147. As of 2018, what is Coach K's record in the Regional Finals (the elite 8 game)?

The Greatest Game Ever Played

Whether you are a Duke fan or not, the Duke-Kentucky regional finals game in 1992 is at least on your top 5 greatest college games of all time. For those of you who saw that game, it is etched in your memory forever.

148. What was the final score of the Duke/Kentucky 1992 Regional Final game?

149. How many seconds were left on the clock when Duke inbounded the ball for the game winning shot?

150. What were Coach K's famous first words to his team at the beginning of the last time-out, down by one point, against Kentucky?

151. How much of what Coach K said and did during that time out do you know?

152. Who made the length of the court pass for that game winning shot?

153. Who made the game winning shot?

154. Can you recall the words of Verne Lundquist on that final play?

155. In what game earlier that season, did Duke try the exact same play to go the length of the court in attempts to win? What happened? Why did it not succeed?

156. Besides the game winning shot against Kentucky, what other team did Duke knock out of the regional finals on a buzzer beating shot from Christian Laettner two years earlier?

157. In which year was Duke ranked #1 in the AP poll every single week of the season? From pre-season all the way to winning the National Title?

158. As of 2018, out of which region has Duke won the most NCAA Tournament games?

    a. East   b. Midwest   C. South   d. West

    e. Southeast   f. Mideast

159. Out of which region does Duke have the highest winning percentage in NCAA Tournament games?

    a. East   b. Midwest   C. South   d. West

    e. Southeast   f. Mideast

160. As of the end of the 2018 season, in which decade does Duke have the most number of NCAA Tournament wins? How many?

161. As of 2018, which team has Duke defeated the most times in the NCAA Tournament? How many times has Duke defeated them in the tournament?

162. Which conference has Duke defeated the most in the NCAA Tournament?

163. In which state has Duke won the most NCAA Tournament games?

164. As of 2018, there have been three states that Duke has played at least one NCAA tournament game in and has never won in that state. Can you name the states?

    1)

    2)

    3)

165. The old saying states that *Defense Wins Championships.* Which Duke team holds the school record for the best scoring defense (post 1951)?

166. The top 4 largest crowds to ever watch a Duke game all happen to come from the same arena. Which basketball venue was it?

167. Who is the career leader in number of NCAA tournament games played? How many NCAA tournament games did he play in?

168. Who is the career leader in number total points scored in the NCAA tournament?

The Championship Years

The 1991 Championship – **After many trips to the Final Four in the previous few years, Duke finally won the whole thing in 1991. Let's look at some facts from that championship team.**

169. In the 1990 NCAA championship, Duke lost to UNLV by an NCAA record number of points. How many points did the Blue Devils lost by?

170. Name the starting 5 for Duke in the 1991 National Championship Game

1)

2)

3)

4)

5)

171. Who were some of the key reserves that played important roles in the 1991 drive to a championship?

172. Who did Duke defeat in the Semi-Final Game in 1991 to move onto the national title game?

173. How many games in a row had their semi-final opponent won before Duke defeated them in the National Semi-final game?

174. What was their semi-final opponent's average margin of victory that year?

175. Who did Duke defeat in the Championship game in 1991?

176. Who was named the Most Outstanding Player for the 1991 Final Four.

177. In what city did Duke win the 1991 Championship?

The 1992 Championship – In one of the most dominant seasons in Duke history, the Blue Devils made it two in a row. Let's look at some facts from that championship team.

178. How many years had it been since a team won back-to-back championships before Duke did it in 1992. Who was the last team to do it before Duke?

179. Since Duke won back-to-back championships in 1991 and 1992, only one other college basketball team has done that (as of 2018). Who was that team?

180. Name the starting 5 for Duke in the 1992 National Championship Game

    1)

    2)

    3)

    4)

    5)

181. Who are some of the key reserves that played important roles in the 1992 drive to a championship?

182. Who did Duke defeat in the Semi-Final Game in 1992 to move onto the national title game?

183. Who did Duke defeat in the Championship game in 1992?

184. Who was named the Most Outstanding Player for the 1992 Final Four.

185. In what city did Duke win the 1991 Championship?

The 2001 Championship – After falling short on a last second shot in the finals in 1999, in what many say is the greatest team to not win a national championship, the 2001 team made amends for that loss to once again bring the championship trophy back to Durham. Let's look at some facts from that championship team.

186. What pre-season tournament did Duke win in the 2000-01 season and who did they defeat in the finals of that tournament?

187. In 2001, Duke shared the ACC regular season title with what team?

188. Who did Duke defeat in the championship game of the ACC Tournament in 2001?

189. Name the starting 5 for Duke in the 2001 National Championship Game

       1)

       2)

       3)

       4)

       5)

190. Who are some of the key reserves that played important roles in the 2001 drive to a championship?

191. Who did Duke defeat in the Semi-Final Game in 2001 to move onto the national title game?

192. Who did Duke defeat in the Championship game in 2001?

193. Who was named the Most Outstanding Player for the 2001 Final Four.

194. In what city did Duke win the 2001 Championship?

The 2010 Championship – For many, the Duke team that won the title in 2010 is the most improbable of all of its championship teams. Yet they brought the fourth championship banner to Cameron Indoor Stadium. Let's look at some facts from that championship team.

195. What was the won/loss record for the seniors on the 2010 championship team when they were freshmen?

196. When the Senior Class of 2010 were freshmen, how many rounds in the NCAA Tournament did they go?

197. When the Senior Class of 2010 were sophomores, how many rounds in the NCAA Tournament did they go?

198. What starting line-up change did Coach K make in the latter half of the 2010 season that propelled the Blue Devils to the championship?

199. Name the starting 5 for Duke in the 2010 National Championship Game

        1)

        2)

        3)

        4)

        5)

200. Who were some of the key reserves that played important roles in the 2010 drive to a championship?

201. Who did Duke defeat in the Semi-Final Game in 2010 to move onto the national title game?

202. Who did Duke defeat in the Championship game in 2010?

203. Who was named the Most Outstanding Player for the 2010 Final Four.

204. In what city did Duke win the 2010 Championship?

The 2015 Championship – **This was a team most noted for three freshmen starters, all one-and-done players, that helped lead the way to Duke's fifth national championship.**

205. Which two freshmen made a pact together several years earlier that they would both play for the same college team?

206. Who was the only senior in the starting line-up of the 2015 season?

207. Which freshman player famously came off the bench to spark a comeback in the title game?

208. Name the starting 5 for Duke in the 2015 National Championship Game

      1)

      2)

      3)

      4)

      5)

209. Who were some of the key reserves that played important roles in the 2015 drive to a championship?

210. Who did Duke defeat in the Semi-Final Game in 2015 to move onto the national title game?

211. Who did Duke defeat in the Championship game in 2015?

212. Who was named the Most Outstanding Player for the 2015 Final Four.

213. In what city did Duke win the 2015 Championship?

DUKE IN THE NBA

214. Name the former Duke Players who have won at least one NBA championship. Circle any players who have won both a NCAA and NBA championship. As of 2017, there have been 5 former Duke players to win at least one NBA championship.

1)

2)

3)

4)

5)

215. Which former Duke players have won NBA rookie of the year? As of 2017 there have been three.

1)

2)

3)

216. Name the former Duke players who have been on an NBA All-Rookie Teams. As of 2017, there have been 13.

1)

2)

3)

4)

5)

6)

7)

8)

9)

10)

11)

12)

13)

217. Which former Duke players have been on the NBA All-Defensive team? As of 2017, there have been two.

   1)

   2)

218. Which former Duke players were the number one selection in the NBA draft? As of 2017, there have been three.

   1)

   2)

   3)

219. Name the Duke former players or assistant coaches who are either assistant or head coaches in the NBA.

220. Name the Duke for players who are in the front office of an NBA team

221. Which former Duke player has won an NBA All-Star game MVP?

222. Which two former NBA head coaches, broadcasters, and Hall of Famers were once Duke assistant coaches?

DUKE TRIVIA CHALLENGE ANSWERS

Jersey Retirements

1. As of 2018, there have been 13 jerseys that hang in the rafters of Cameron. List the Players and Their Numbers Who have had their jerseys retired.

  1) #10 - Dick Groat

  2) #25 - Art Heyman

  3) #44 - Jeff Mullins

  4) #43 - Mike Gminski

  5) #24 - Johnny Dawkins

  6) #35 - Danny Ferry

  7) #32 - Christian Laettner

  8) #11 - Bobby Hurley

  9) #33 - Grant Hill

  10) #31 - Shane Battier

  11) #22 - Jason Williams

  12) #23 - Shelden Williams

  13) #4 - J.J. Redick

Player of the Year Awards

2. As if 2018, there have been six different Duke players named National Defensive Player of the Year. Who were they?

   1) Tommy Amaker   4) Steve Wojciechowski

   2) Billy King   5) Shane Battier

   3) Grant Hill   6) Sheldon Williams

3. Which Duke player was named National Defensive Player of the year in three different seasons?

Shane Battier

4. As of 2018, there have been 9 Duke players name National Player of the Year. Can you name them (7 have been in the Coach K era)?

   1) Dick Groat   6) Elton Brand

   2) Art Heyman   7) Shane Battier

   3) Johnny Dawkins   8) Jason Williams

   4) Danny Ferry   9) J.J. Redick

   5) Christian Laettner

5. Name the only two Duke players who have won National Player of the Year in two different seasons

   1) Jason Williams   2) J.J. Redick

6. As of 2018, there have been 3 Duke freshmen who have won the National Freshman of the Year Award. Who are they?

1) Luol Deng

2) Jabari Parker

3) Jahlil Okafor

7. As of 2018, there have been 14 Duke players named ACC Player of the Year. Without looking it up, how many can you name?

1) Art Heyman	*8) Elton Brand*
2) Jeff Mullins	*9) Chris Carrawell*
3) Steve Vacendak	*10) Shane Battier*
4) Mike Gminski	*11) J.J. Redick*
5) Danny Ferry	*12) Nolan Smith*
6) Christian Laettner	*13) Jahil Okafor*
7) Grant Hill	*14) Marvin Bagley III*

8. Which two players have won ACC player of the year in two different years?

1) Danny Ferry *2) J.J. Redick*

9. As of 2018, there have been 10 Duke freshmen that have been named ACC Freshman of the Year. How many can you name without looking it up?

1) Jim Spanarkel   *6) Austin Rivers*

2) Mike Gminski   *7) Jabari Parker*

3) Gene Banks   *8) Jahil Okafor*

4) Chris Duhon   *9) Brandon Ingram*

5) Kyle Singler   *10) Marvin Bagley III*

10. As of 2018, there have only been two players in ACC history who have been named both ACC Freshman of the Year and ACC Player of the Year in the same season. Who were they?

1) Jahil Okafor   *2) Marvin Bagley III*

Duke Records

11. Who is Duke's career leader in number of games played?

Amile Jefferson played 150 games with Duke

12. Who is Duke's career leader in minutes played?

Kyle Singler played 4,887 minutes while at Duke

13. Who holds the freshman scoring record at Duke?

Marvin Bagley III scored 694 points as a freshman

14. Who holds the freshman rebounding record at Duke?

Marvin Bagley III had 366 rebounds as a freshman

15. Who is Duke's all-time scoring leader?

J.J. Redick with 2,769 points

16. Who is Duke's all-time assist leader?

Bobby Hurley with 1,076 assists

17. Who is Duke's all-time leader in rebounds?

Sheldon Williams with 1262 rebounds

18. Who is Duke's all-time leader in steals?

Christ Duhon with 301

19. Who is Duke's all-time leader in blocks?

Sheldon Williams with 422

20. Who is Duke's all-time leader in Free throw percentage?

J.J. Redick 91.2 %

21. Who is Duke's all-time leader in 3 point percentage (minimums 70 attempts)?

Christian Laettner with 48.5%

22. Who is Duke all-time leader in field goal percentage?

Carlos Boozer 63.1%

23. Who is Duke's all-time leader in charges taken?

Shane Battier with 111

24. Who has the most dunks in Duke history?

Mason Plumlee with 217 dunks

25. Which two players share the Duke record for most three point shots made in a game?

1) Shane Battier   2) J.J. Redick

They each hit 9 three pointers in a game

26. Which two players share the record for the most blocked shots in a single game? How many did they each block?

1) Cherokee Parks   2) Sheldon Williams

They each had a 10 block shot game

27. Who holds the Duke record for most assists in a game? How many assists did he have?

Bobby Hurley had 16 assists in a single game

MY PERSONAL ALL-TIME LISTS
OF GREAT DUKE PLAYERS

The following is my personal list. It doesn't mean that my list is any better than your list. For various reasons, these are the players that I would choose.

28. If you could add a jersey (or two) to hang from the rafters of Cameron, who would you add and why?

Kyle Singler, Grayson Allen

But technically, neither fit the pre-determined standard that they both graduate and receive some kind of national player of the year award. With that criteria, I don't think anyone will ever have their jersey retired again. The player of the year winners will all leave before they graduate.

29. What Duke players or coaches have you personally met?

Coach K at a book signing

Chris Collins and Jeff Capel when they were players at the US Olympic Festival as players.

Justin Robinson at church in San Antonio

30. Who is your number one all-time favorite Duke player and why?

This was perhaps the hardest one for me personally to answer. I am tempted to go with a 3-way tie between Christian Laettner, Bobby Hurley, and Shane Battier.

But if I had to narrow it down to only one player, it would have to be

Christian Laettner (I sure hate to eliminate those other two). Two national championships, game winning shots, Four Final Fours. In my opinion, the greatest competitor to wear the Duke uniform.

Name your personal All-Time List of Duke Players (for me personally, I am not putting any one and done players on this list. To be an All-Time Great on my list, they had to have a larger body of work than just a single year.

31. **First Team**

PG	*Bobby Hurley*	*– competitor, true point guard, assist record holder*
Wing	*J.J. Redick*	*– three point king, Duke's all-time leading scorer*
Wing	*Grant Hill*	*– he could do it all*
Post	*Shane Battier*	*– perhaps both the best defensive player and the best leader Duke has ever had.*
Post	*Christian Laettner*	*– in my opinion the greatest competitor ever to wear the Duke uniform. Clutch Player. Refused to lose.*

32. **Second Team**

PG	*Jayson Williams*	*– could handle the ball, could score, could lead the break. Miracle Minute (need I say more)*
Wing	*Grayson Allen*	
Wing	*Chris Duhon*	
Post	*Elton Brand*	
Post	*Sheldon Williams*	

33. **Third Team**

PG	*Quin Snyder*
Wing	*Kyle Singler*
Wing	*Nolan Smith*
Post	*Carlos Boozer*
Post	*Mason Plumlee*

34. Who is your All-Time Freshman team (does not have to be a one and done player, but can be)? I chose not to put Kyrie Irving on my list because I wanted players with more than 11 games to qualify.

PG	*Tyus Jones*
Wing	*Justice Winslow*
Wing	*Luol Deng*
Post	*Marvin Bagley III*
Post	*Jahil Okafer*
Other	*Wendell Carter*
Other	*Gary Trent, Jr.*

35. Who is your All-Time 4 year player team?

PG	*Bobby Hurley*
Wing	*J.J. Redick*
Wing	*Grant Hill*
Post	*Shane Battier*

Post	*Christian Laettner*
Other	*Sheldon Williams*
Other	*Kyle Singler*

Your All Decade Teams

36. 1970's   I never saw any of these players play so I really cannot fill out this list.

PG

Wing

Wing

Post

Post

Other

Other

37. *1980's*

PG	*Quin Snyder*
Wing	*Johnny Dawkins*
Wing	*Billy King*
Post	*Danny Ferry*
Post	*Alaa Abdelnaby*
Other	*Tommy Amaker*
Other	*Jay Bilas*

38. **1990's**

PG	*Bobby Hurley*
Wing	*Grant Hill*
Wing	*Trejan Langdon*
Post	*Christian Laettner*
Post	*Shane Battier*
Other	*Elton Brand*
Other	*Chris Collins*

39. **2000-2009**

PG	*Jason Williams*
Wing	*J.J. Redick*
Wing	*Kyle Singler*
Post	*Carlos Boozer*
Post	*Sheldon Williams*
Other	*Chris Duhon*
Other	*Nolan Smith*

40. 2010-2018 (at publication time)

PG	*Tyus Jones*
Wing	*Justice Winslow*
Wing	*Grayson Allen*
Post	*Marvin Bagley III*
Post	*Jahil Okafer*
Other	*Wendell Carter*
Other	*Quin Cook*

BY THE NUMBERS

41. Name at least one player who has worn each number in a Duke uniform. I am choosing my favorite player with each number, but in some cases I might choose more than one.

#0   *Jayson Tatum* (I never liked Austin Rivers so I can't include him)

#1   *Jabari Parker, Kyrie Irving*

#2   *Quin Cook, Nolan Smith*

#3   *Grayson Allen*

#4   *JJ Redick* (Carlos Boozer, Tommy Amaker)

#5   Tyus Jones, Luke Kennard, Mason Plumlee

#10 *Dick Groat* (never saw him play)

#11 *Bobby Hurley*

#12 *Steve Wojciechowski, Kyle Singler, Justise Winslow, Thomas Hill*

#13 *Matt Jones*

#14 *Quin Snyder*

#15 *Jahlil Okafor*

#20 *Chris Collins,*

#21 Chris Duhon, Trajan Langdon

#22 Jason Williams

#23 Shelden Williams, Chris Carrawell, Brian Davis

#24 Johnny Dawkins

#25 Art Heyman (never saw him play)

#30 Jon Scheyer

#31 Shane Battier

#32 Christian Laettner

#33 Grant Hill

#34 Mike Dunleavy, Wendell Carter

#35 Danny Ferry, Marvin Bagley

#40 Marshall Plumlee

#41 Matt Christensen

#42 Elton Brand

#43 Mike Gminski (never saw him play)

#44 Cherokee Parks

#45 Clay Buckley

#50 Justin Robinson, Corey Maggette

#51 Mike Buckmire

#52 Erik Meek

#53 Brennan Besser

#54 Christian Ast

#55 Billy King, Brian Zoubek

42. What was the highest scoring average for any Duke team? How many points did they average?

The 1964-65 team averaged 92.4 ppg.

In the Coach K era, the 1998-99 team averaged 91.8 ppg

43. What is the most number of wins in a season by a Duke team?

Twice Duke has won 37 games in a season. Ironically, both times (1986 and 1999, they lost in the national semi-finals

44. What is the most points one player scored in a single game in Duke history? Who did it and how many points did he score?

Danny Ferry holds the school record with 58 points on December 10, 1988 against Miami.

45. What year was a Coach K led Duke team first ranked in the top 10 in the Final AP Poll?

Duke finished the season ranked tenth in the 1985 season.

46. What year did Duke play its first basketball game?

1905

BY THE NAMES

47. Here is a challenge for you. Out of the 26 letters in the alphabet, how many can you attach to the last name of a Duke basketball player? Every letter might not have a last name associated with it and in that case, you could use a first name.

A. *Grayson Allen*

B. *Shane Battier*

C. *Chris Collins*

D. *Johnny Dawkins*

E. *Daniel Ewing*

F. *Danny Ferry*

G. *Mike Gminski*

H. *Grant Hill, Bobby Hurley*

I. *Kyrie Irving*

J. *Nate James*

K. *Billy King*

L. *Christian Laettner*

M. Jeff Mullins

N. Demarcus Nelson

O. Jahlil Okafor

P. Mason Plumlee

Q. Quinn Snyder

R. JJ Reddick

S. Kyle Singler

T. Lance Thomas

U. Bill Ulrich – The only Duke player whose last name started with U

V. Antonio Vrankovic

W. Jason Williams

X.

Y. Kenny Young – Never heard of him, but he played in 1975-76

Z. Brian Zoubek

48. Which former Duke player became President Obama's personal trainer?

Reggie Love

Nicknames

49. Who was *The Alaskan Assassin?*

Trajan Langdon

50. What player did the Duke fans affectionally call *Chief?*

Cherokee Parks

51. Who was *The Minister of Defense?*

Shane Battier

52. Who was termed *The Landlord?*

Sheldon Williams

53. Who was nicknamed *Tinkerbell?*

Gene Banks

54. Who was known as the *Gman?*

Mike Gminski

Other Name Related Trivia

55. What was the original name of Duke University?

This answer is actually multi-faceted. In 1938, Brown Schoolhouse was founded in Randolph County, NC. In 1859, it was renamed Trinity College. In 1892, the college moved to Durham, NC and in 1924, was founded as Duke University

.56. What Duke player had a father who was a former All-pro NFL running back?

Grant Hill's father, Calvin Hill was a long time NFL running back.

57. What three brothers have won national championships at Duke?

Miles and Mason Plumlee played on the 2010 Duke National Championship team

Younger brother Marshall played on the 2015 Duke National Championship team.

58. What organization was the inspiration behind naming the mascot, *Blue Devils?*

A well-known battalion of French soldiers known as "les Diables Bleus" was the inspiration behind the name Blue Devils

59. Who actually decided to name the mascot the *Blue Devils?*

The student editors on the 1922-1923 Trinity Chronicle began referring to their teams as the Blue Devils. The name stuck.

60. Who is Duke University named after?

After the then Trinity College received a very large endowment from tobacco tycoon James B. Duke, the college's president, William Preston Few chose to rename the college, Duke University. James. B. Duke agreed under the condition that it be named after his father and family – hence the name Duke and not a first name associated with it.

61. The One and Done Rule officially began on in 2006, who was Duke's first official one and done player?

Kyrie Irving. Though he was not the first Duke Player to declare for the NBA draft after his freshman year, the others came before the NBA instituted the rule that a player must be one year removed from graduation from high school

62. What Duke assistant coaches have won the NCAA National Championship both as a player and a coach?

As of 2018, two of Duke's assistant coaches have won national championships as both a player and assistant coach.

> *Nate James won as a player in 2001 and an assistant coach in both 2010 and 2015*

> *John Scheyer won as a player in 2010 and an assistant coach in 2015.*

63. In the history of Duke basketball, there have been 3 father/son combinations that played for Duke. Who are they? If you know of any others, let me know and I will change it.

David and Alex O'Connell

Jay and Clay Buckley

Gary and Lee Melchionni

64. What do the Duke players do to signify that they are going to make a stand on defense?

Slap the floor.

COACH K

65. Of what national decent did Coach K come from?

Polish

66. What did Coach K's father do for a living?

Elevator Operator

67. What kind of work did his mother do?

Cleaned floors at the Chicago Athletic Center

68. Coach K has always talked about his older brother being his hero. What did Bill K do for a living?

Fireman

69. What did Coach K's friends call him when he was growing up?

Mickie

70. What is Coach K's wife name?

Mickie

71. How many daughters does Coach K have? Can you name them?

Coach K has three daughters. Debbie Savarino, Lindy Frasher, and Jamie Spatola)

72. How many grandchildren does Coach K have?

Ten grandchildren

73. Where did Coach K coach before taking the Duke job?

Army

74. As a graduate assistant coach, who did Coach K coach under for a year?

Bobby Knight

75. What was Coach K's rank in the army?

Captain

76. How many wins did Coach K have prior to coming to Duke?

While at Army Coach had a total coaching record of 73-59

77. Who recommended Coach K to then Duke Athletic Director Tom Butters?

Bobby Knight

78. Who was Coach K's very first prize recruit?

Johnny Dawkins

79. What infamous loss early in his Duke tenure, prompted Coach K to say, "Here's to never forgetting."

In 1983, after suffering a humiliating loss to Virginia by 43 points, the Blue Devil coaching staff and sports information director were eating when Johnny More proposed a toast saying, "Here's to forgetting tonight ever happened." Coach K interrupted and said, "Here's to never forgetting." As if he was prophetic, Duke did not lost again to Virginia for 16 games.

80. How many times has Coach K won the National Coach of the Year Award? Can you name the years?

Coach K has won the NCAA National Coach of the Year 8 times - 1986, 1989, 1991, 1992, 1997, 1999, 2000, 2001

81. How many times has Coach K won the ACC Coach of the Year Award? Can you name the years?

Coach K has won ACC Coach of the Year 5 times 1984, 1986, 1997, 1999, 2000

82. Who was Duke playing when Coach K became the winningest coach in NCAA men's basketball history?

On November 15, 2011, Duke defeated Michigan State to give Coach K his 903rd victory, breaking his mentor's record of 902 to become the NCAA Division 1 All-time win leader.

83. Where was Duke playing when Coach K became the winningest coach in NCAA men's basketball history?

Other than winning the game at Cameron, Coach K's 903rd win was fittingly won in perhaps the world's most famous basketball arena – Madison Square Garden

84. Who was Duke playing when Coach K won his 1000th game?

On January 25, 2015, Duke defeated St. Johns to give him 1000 career wins.

85. Where was Duke playing when Coach K won his 1000th game?

Fittingly enough, just as he did when he became the winningest coach in NCAA history, Coach K won his 1000th game at Madison Square Garden

86. Who was Duke playing when Coach K won his 1000th game as the coach at Duke?

On November 11, 2017, Coach K won his 100th game as the Duke coach when Duke defeated Utah Valley

87. Where was Duke playing when Coach won his 1000th game as the coach at Duke?

Finally, Coach K reached one of those great milestones in front of the home crowd at Cameron Indoor Stadium

88. What is Coach K's overall international record in coaching TEAM USA?

88-1

89. Where is Coach K's office?

Coach K's office is located on the top floor of the tower that is connected to Cameron Indoor Stadium by a hallway that leads to the Duke Basketball Museum. His office overlooks K-Ville.

90. What iconic symbol of Coach K's basketball philosophy is engraved into the 2001 National Championship ring? It is also a sculpture in his office?

The FIST

91. This symbol is also an acronym. What does it stand for?

Five Individuals Standing Together

92. Name the only college basketball teams that Coach K has a losing record against while at Duke (Hint: As of 2018, there are only 4)

Arizona 3-5   Louisville 5-6

California 1-2   Arkansas 1-2

93. When was Coach K inducted into the Basketball Hall of Fame?

On October 5, 2001, Coach K was inducted into the Naismith Basketball Hall of Fame.

94. Who was the first number one ranked team that Coach K beat?

On March 10. 1984, in the ACC Semi-Finals, Duke defeated North Carolina, 77-75, to give Coach K his first win against a number one ranked opponent.

DUKE UNIVERSITY AND CAMERON INDOOR STADIUM

95. What are the Duke basketball fans called in their home games?

The Cameron Crazies

96. What two words do the fans chant at Cameron when the opposing player who just fouled out sits down?

When an opposing player fouls out, the Cameron Crazies stand and jeer the person with a loud rumble until that player sits down. As soon as he sits, the Crazies say in unison, "See ya"

97. What bust famously sits outside Cameron Indoor Stadium?

Eddie Cameron, the former head basketball coach who the arena was named for.

98. What year was Cameron Indoor Stadium built?

1940

99. What is the current seating/standing capacity of Cameron?

The official capacity of Cameron Indoor Stadium is 9,314.

100. What is the song sung during every game in Cameron that the crowd jumps up and down during the chorus? Fill in the blanks.

"__Every time__ we __touch__"

101. According to legend, what did Eddie Cameron and Wallace Wade use to sketch and design the basketball stadium?

A Match Box

102. What was the original name of Cameron Indoor Stadium?

Duke Indoor Stadium

103. What year was the stadium renamed Cameron Indoor Stadium?

1972

104. Who was the opponent for the game when the stadium was officially renamed Cameron Indoor Stadium?

On January 22, 1972, the stadium was officially renamed Cameron Indoor Stadium in a game that Duke beat #3 ranked North Carolina on a last second shot.

105. In what game did the now famous chant "air ball" originate?

Late in the first half on February 24, 1979, UNC's Rich Yonakor shot an air ball. According to legend, for the rest of his career, the Cameron Crazies taunted him each time he touched the ball by using a relentless chant of "air bal.l" Though this fact is not official, it is widely accepted that it was this game that the famous chant of "air ball" originated.

106. How many different players recruited by Coach K and stayed four years never were part of a team that hung a banner in the rafters?

If you count winning regular season ACC champions (it wasn't recognized for a long time), only three of Coach K's recruits who stayed four years have not won something worthy of a banner in Cameron. They all came from the 1981-82 recruiting class (Coach K's first recruits at Duke) never won any kind of championship. As of 2018, every other player who has stayed four years have won at least one.

107. In what year was the basketball court inside Cameron Indoor Stadium officially named *Coach K Court*

On November 17, 2000, moments after Coach won his 500th victory, he was surprised with a ceremony naming the basketball court inside Cameron, Coach K Court.

108. How was the initial building of the stadium initially funded?

    a. Gifts from boosters?
    b. Duke football team's Rose Bowl earnings
    c. Fund raisers by the athletic department
    d. Money earned from Television royalties

109. What is the most consecutive number of victories at Cameron?

From Jan. 13, 1997 – Feb. 9, 2000, Duke won a total of 46 home games in a row.

110. Three different years, Duke has won 17 games at Cameron. Which years did they accomplish this?

2010, 2011, 2014

111. Describe where is Krzyzewskiville located?

Krzyzewskiville, the famous grassy area that sits behind Cameron Indoor Stadium is the place where students camp out sometimes for weeks before a big game. Coach K's office overlooks Krzyzewskiville.

112. How many can occupy a single tent in Krzyzewskiville?

12

113. What year did Krzyzewskiville begin?

Unofficially, K-ville began in 1986, the Thursday before Duke played host to North Carolina when 15 friends decided to camp out in 4 tents before the game. By the time the Saturday game tipped off, there were 75 tents camped outside Cameron.

114. How many total tents are allowed in K-ville??

100

115. In a group is registered at *black registration (*the first wave*)*, how many people must occupy a tent at any time during the day?

2 Tent members must be there for the day time hours, which is considered to be between 7:00AM and 2:20AM

116. In a group is registered at *black registration (*the first wave*)*, how many people must occupy a tent at night?

10 Tent members must be there for the day time hours, which is considered to be between 2:30 AM and 7:00 AM

117. Just because you want to camp in Krzyzewskiville doesn't mean you automatically get to. How do they determine if you get in and where your tent is located?

First you have to be one of the first 100 groups to sign up. The order of where your tent is determined by a Duke trivia test.

118. Who is credited for the beginning of K-ville?

Kimberly Reed

ACC RIVALS AND OTHER FAMOUS GAMES

119. Other than Durham, what city has Duke won the most games in?

As of 2018, Duke has won more games (33) in Raleigh, North Carolina against NC State than any other city.

120. Other than Coach K, list your personal five all-time favorite ACC coaches (this is my list)

1) Jim Valvano

2) Bobby Cremmins

3) Gary Williams

4) Dave Odem

5) Tony Bennett

121. How many ACC schools does Duke NOT hold an all-time head to head advantage with? Name them?

The North Carolina Tarheels are the only ACC team to hold a winning record against Duke

122. What is Duke's won/loss record against UNC during the Coach K era?

As of 2018, Coach K holds a 46-42 record over UNC. During that time, UNC has had 4 different head coaches

123. What ACC team does Duke have the most all-time victories against?

North Carolina State

124. Usually, in the last home game of the year, also known as Senior Night, Coach K likes to take his Seniors out of the game in the final minute so they can receive one last cheer from the home crowd. However, sometimes due to the closeness of the game, he doesn't have the opportunity to do that. In his final home game on Senior Night, as time expired in a two-point come from behind victory, which player made a beeline sprint straight to Coach K giving him a big hug? Hint: It is still often shown on ESPN highlights.

Steve Wojciechowski

125. Besides Bobby Hurley who is the number one assist man in ACC history, which other Blue Devil is ranked in the top 5 in the ACC in career assists?

Chris Duhon is ranked 5th in the All-Time Assist leader list in the ACC.

126. Who holds the record for the most number of ACC wins in a career?

In his career, Shane Battier won with 70 ACC victories

127. As of the tournament in 2018, how many ACC tournaments has Duke won?

20 ACC tournament titles

128. What year was the ACC formed and who were the founding members?

Year – 1953

    1) Clemson

    2) Duke

    3) Maryland

    4) North Carolina

    5) North Carolina State

    6) South Carolina

    7) Wake Forest

129. How far apart are the campuses of Duke and North Carolina?

Officially, the two campuses are ten miles apart

130. What is the nickname given to "road" that runs from Duke to UNC to NC State?

Tobacco Road

131. In his final home game, what did Gene Banks throw into the crowd?

Roses

132. How many conferences does Duke have a losing record against?

Duke does not have a losing record against any conference

133. Other than the ACC, which conference does Duke have the most number of wins against?

As of 2018, Duke has 197 victories against Big 10 opponents, by far the most against any conference other than the ACC.

134. Duke holds the ACC record with the most consecutive ACC Tournament titles. How many years in a row did the win it?

Between 1999-2003, Duke won 5 consecutive ACC Tournament titles.

135. Duke holds the ACC record for most consecutive ACC victories. What year(s) did they accomplish this and how long was the streak?

Duke won 31 consecutive ACC games between Feb. 8, 1998 and Feb. 9, 2000

136. Duke holds the ACC record for most consecutive ACC **road** victories. What year(s) did they accomplish this and how long was the streak?

Duke won 24 consecutive conference road victories from February 1998 to February 2001

137. What was Duke's largest margin of victory ever?

Technically, it happened in 1910 as Duke beat Furman, 85-5. But if we look only at the modern era of basketball, Duke beat Harvard 130-54 (76 points) on November 25, 1989

138. What was the biggest halftime deficit that Duke has come back from to win and who was the opponent? (this is not an ACC game)

Duke holds the NCAA record for the largest halftime deficit in which the team came back to win. On Dec. 30, 1950, Duke trailed Tulane 56-27 at halftime. They came back to win the game 74-72

139. Who hit a buzzer beating three-point shot in 2012 to beat UNC?

Austin Rivers

140. What was the deficit in the final minute of the road game against Maryland before the comeback known as *The Miracle Minute* took place?

In what should have been an sure Maryland victory, Duke trailed by 10 points with under a minute to play, but forced overtime and won the game in overtime.

141. In 1979, Duke held UNC scoreless for the entire first half. What was the halftime score and what was the final score of the game?

With North Carolina going into the four corners offense to start the game and playing it throughout the entire first half, Duke took a 7-0 lead into halftime. The final score was 47-40 Duke.

142. As of 2018, only one ACC team had each of their five starters named to an All-ACC team? Which Duke team accomplish this? Name the five players.

The 1999 Duke basketball team put all 5 of their starters on one of the All-ACC teams.

1) *Elton Brand (1st)*

2) *Trajan Langdon (1st)*

3) *William Avery (2nd)*

4) *Shane Battier (3rd)*

5) *Chris Carrawell (3rd)*

THE NCAA TOURNAMENT

143. What year did a Coach K coached Duke receive its first NCAA Tournament bid?

1984. They lost in the second round.

144. What year did Duke first play in the Final Four?

1963

145. There have been three players in NCAA history that have played in four Final Fours. Who were they?

1) Greg Koubek

2) Christian Laettner

3) Brian Davis

146. What was the largest deficit Duke had in the 2001 National Semi-final game against Maryland before coming back to win it?

22 points

147. As of 2018, what is Coach K's record in the Regional Finals (the elite 8 game)?

12-3

148. What was the final score of the Duke/Kentucky 1992 Regional Final game?

104-103

149. How many second were left on the clock when Duke inbounded the ball for the game winning shot?

2.1 seconds

150. What were Coach K's famous first words to his team at the beginning of the last time-out, down by one point, against Kentucky?

"We're going to win."

151. How much of what Coach K said and did during that time out do you know?

Besides his statement that they were going to win, Coach asked Grant Hill if he could make the pass. Then he asked Christian Laettner if he could catch the pass.

152. Who made the length of the court pass for that game winning shot?

Grant Hill

153. Who made the game winning shot?

Christian Laettner

154. Can you recall the words of Verne Lundquist on that final play?

"There's the pass to Laettner ... puts it up ... YES!"

155. In what game earlier that season, did Duke try the exact same play to go the length of the court in attempts to win? What happened? Why did it not succeed?

In a game at Wake Forest earlier in the season, Duke tried the exact same play. However, Grant Hill's pass sailed to the sideline and when Laettner caught it, he stepped out of bounds.

156. Besides the game winning shot against Kentucky, what other team did Duke knock out of the regional finals on a buzzer beating shot from Christian Laettner two years earlier?

Duke knocked out the Connecticut Huskies in the 1990 regional finals on a Christian Laettner last second shot.

157. In which year was Duke ranked #1 in the AP poll every single week of the season? From pre-season all the way to winning the National Title.

1991-92

158. As of 2018, out of which region has Duke won the most NCAA Tournament games?

a. East   b. Midwest   C. South   d. West

e. Southeast   f. Mideast

159. Out of which region does Duke have the highest winning percentage in NCAA Tournament games?

    a. East   b. Midwest   **C. South**   d. West

    e. Southeast   f. Mideast

160. As of the end of the 2018 season, in which decade does Duke have the most number of NCAA Tournament wins? How many?

In the 1990's Duke had an overall NCAA tournament record of 32-7

161. As of 2018, which team has Duke defeated the most times in the NCAA Tournament? How many times has Duke defeated them in the tournament?

Duke has defeated Michigan State 5 times in the NCAA Tournament

162. Which conference has Duke defeated the most in the NCAA Tournament?

The Big 10

163. In which state has Duke won the most NCAA Tournament games?

As of 2018, Duke is 34-6 in the NCAA Tournament in their home state of North Carolina

164. As of 2018, there have been three states that Duke has played at least one NCAA tournament game in and has never won in that state. Can you name the states?

1) *California*

2) *Ohio*

3) *Washington*

165. The old saying states that *Defense Wins Championships.* Which Duke team holds the school record for the best scoring defense (post 1951)?

The 2009-2010 team held opponents to 61 points per game

166. The top 4 largest crowds to ever watch a Duke game all happen to come from the same arena. Which basketball venue was it?

In Four Final Four game at Lucas Oil Field in Indianapolis, Duke had crowds watching the game that exceeded 70,000.

On April 4, 2015, 72,238 people were in attendance to watch Duke beat Michigan State.

On April 6, 2015, 71,149 people were in attendance to watch Duke beat Wisconsin

On April 3, 2010, 71,298 people were in attendance to watch Duke beat West Virginia

On April 5, 2010, 70,930 people were in attendance to watch Duke beat Butler

167. Who is the career leader in number of NCAA tournament games played? How many NCAA tournament games did he play in?

In a record that will probably never be broken, Christian Laettner played in 23 career NCAA tournament games.

168. Who is the career leader in number total points scored in the NCAA tournament?

Christian Laettner hold the NCAA Tournament record for most points scored in a career with 407

169. In the 1990 NCAA championship, Duke lost to UNLV by an NCAA record number of points. How many points did the Blue Devils lost by?

Duke lost to UNLV in the 1990 finals by an NCAA finals record 30 points.

170. Name the starting 5 for Duke in the 1991 National Championship Game

1) *Bobby Hurley*

2) *Grant Hill*

3) *Christian Laettner*

4) *Thomas Hill*

5) *Bill McCaffrey*

171. Who were some of the key reserves that played important roles in the 1991 drive to a championship?

Brian Davis, Greg Koubek, Antonio Lang, Crawford Palmer, Marty Clark, Christian Ast, Clay Buckley

172. Who did Duke defeat in the Semi-Final Game in 1991 to move onto the national title game?

UNLV

173. How many games in a row had their semi-final opponent won before Duke defeated them in the National Semi-final game?

Before losing to Duke in the national semi-finals, UNLV had won 45 games in a row.

174. What was their semi-final opponent's average margin of victory that year?

Before their loss to Duke, UNLV's average margin of victory was 27 points per game.

175. Who did Duke defeat in the Championship game in 1991?

Kansas

176. Who was named the Most Outstanding Player for the 1991 Final Four.

Christian Laettner

177. In what city did Duke win the 1991 Championship?

Indianapolis, Indiana

178. How many years had it been since a team won back-to-back championships before Duke did it in 1992. Who was the last team to do it before Duke?

It has been 19 years since UCLA won the last back to back NCAA Championships

179. Since Duke won back-to-back championships in 1991 and 1992, only one other college basketball team has done that (as of 2018). Who was that team?

Florida

180. Name the starting 5 for Duke in the 1992 National Championship Game

    1) Bobby Hurley

    2) Thomas Hill

    3) Brian Davis

    4) Grant Hill

    5) Christian Laettner

181. Who are some of the key reserves that played important roles in the 1992 drive to a championship?

Antonio Lang, Cherokee Park, Marty Clark, Ron Burt, Erik Meek, Kenny Blakeney, Christian Ast

182. Who did Duke defeat in the Semi-Final Game in 1992 to move onto the national title game?

Indiana Hoosiers

183. Who did Duke defeat in the Championship game in 1992?

Michigan Wolverines

184. Who was named the Most Outstanding Player for the 1992 Final Four.

Bobby Hurley

185. In what city did Duke win the 1991 Championship?

Minneapolis, Minnesota

186. What pre-season tournament did Duke win in the 2000-01 season and who did they defeat in the finals of that tournament?

The Pre-Season NIT Tournament

187. In 2001, Duke shared the ACC regular season title with what team?

North Carolina

188. Who did Duke defeat in the championship game of the ACC Tournament in 2001?

North Carolina

189. Name the starting 5 for Duke in the 2001 National Championship Game

    1) Jason Williams

    2) Shame Battier

    3) Mike Dunleavy

    4) Christ Duhon

    5) Casey Sanders (Carlos Boozer was coming off the bench due to just coming back from an injury.

190. Who are some of the key reserves that played important roles in the 2001 drive to a championship?

Carolos Boozer, Nate James

191. Who did Duke defeat in the Semi-Final Game in 2001 to move onto the national title game?

Maryland. It was the fourth time that year that Duke played Maryland

192. Who did Duke defeat in the Championship game in 2001?

Arizona

193. Who was named the Most Outstanding Player for the 2001 Final Four.

Shane Battier

194. In what city did Duke win the 2001 Championship?

Minneapolis, Minesota

195. What was the won/loss record for the seniors on the 2010 championship team when they were freshmen?

They were 22-11, 8-8 in the ACC

196. When the Senior Class of 2010 were freshmen, how many rounds in the NCAA Tournament did they go?

They lost in the first round of the NCAA Tournament

197. When the Senior Class of 2010 were sophomores, how many rounds in the NCAA Tournament did they go?

They lost in the second round of the NCAA Tournament

198. What starting line-up change did Coach K make in the latter half of the 2010 season that propelled the Blue Devils to the championship?

Brian Zoubek was inserted into the starting line-up.

199. Name the starting 5 for Duke in the 2010 National Championship Game

   1) John Scheyer

   2) Kyle Singler

   3) Nolan Smith

   4) Lance Thomas

   5) Brian Zoubek

200. Who were some of the key reserves that played important roles in the 2010 drive to a championship?

Miles Plumlee, Mason Plumlee, Andre Dawkins

201. Who did Duke defeat in the Semi-Final Game in 2010 to move onto the national title game?

West Virginia

202. Who did Duke defeat in the Championship game in 2010?

Butler

203. Who was named the Most Outstanding Player for the 2010 Final Four.

Kyle Singler

204. In what city did Duke win the 2010 Championship?

Indianapolis, Indiana

205. Which two freshmen made a pact together several years earlier that they would both play for the same college team?

Tyus Jones, Jahlil Okafor

206. Who was the only senior in the starting line-up of the 2015 season?

Quin Cook

207. Which freshman player famously came off the bench to spark a comeback in the title game?

Grayson Allen

208. Name the starting 5 for Duke in the 2015 National Championship Game

    1) Tyus Jones

    2) Quinn Cook

    3) Justise Winslow

    4) Jahlil Okafor

    5) Matt Jones

209. Who were some of the key reserves that played important roles in the 2015 drive to a championship?

Amile Jefferson, Marshall Plumlee, Grayson Allen

210. Who did Duke defeat in the Semi-Final Game in 2015 to move onto the national title game?

Michigan State

211. Who did Duke defeat in the Championship game in 2015?

Butler

212. Who was named the Most Outstanding Player for the 2015 Final Four.

Tyus Jones

213. In what city did Duke win the 2015 Championship?

Indianapolis, Indiana

DUKE IN THE NBA

214. Name the former Duke Players who have won at least one NBA championship. Circle any players who have won both a NCAA and NBA championship. As of 2017, there have been 5 former Duke players to win at least one NBA championship.

   1)   Jeff Mullins won in 1975 with Golden State

   2)   Danny Ferry won it in 2003 with San Antonio

   3)   Shame Battier won it in 2012 and 2013 with Miami

   4)   Kyrie Irving won it in 2016 with Cleveland

   5)   Dahntay Jones won it in 2016 with Cleveland

215. Which former Duke players have won NBA rookie of the year? As of 2017 there have been three.

   1)   Grant Hill   1994

   2)   Elton Brand   2000

   3)   Kyrie Irving   2012

216. Name the former Duke players who have been on the NBA All-Rookie Teams. As of 2017, there have been 13.

   1)   Art Heyman   (1st)   1964

   2)   Jack Marin   (1st)   1967

   3)   Christian Laettner (1st)   1993

   4)   Grant Hill   (1st)   1995

   5)   Elton Brand   (1st)   2000

6)	Shane Battier	(1st)	2002
7)	Luol Deng	(1st)	2005
8)	Kyrie Irving	(1st)	2012
9)	Kyle Singler	(2nd)	2013
10)	Mason Plumlee	(1st)	2014
11)	Jahlil Okafor	(1st)	2016
12)	Justise Winslow	(2nd)	2016
13)	Brandon Ingram	(2nd)	2017

217. Which former Duke players have been on the NBA All-Defensive team? As of 2017, there have been two.

| 1) | Shame Battier | (2nd) | 2008, 2009 |
| 2) | Luol Deng | (2nd) | 2012 |

218. Which former Duke players were the number one selection in the NBA draft? As of 2017, there have been three.

1)	Art Heyman	New York Knicks	1963
2)	Elton Brand	Chicago Bulls	1999
3)	Kyrie Irving	Cleveland Cavaliers	2011

219. Name the Duke former players or assistant coaches who are either assistant or head coaches in the NBA (as of 2018)

Chip Engelland – Assistant with San Antonio

Quin Synder – Head Coach Utah

Antonio Lang – Assistant with Utah

Sheldon Williams – Scout with Brooklyn

Dave McClure – Assistant with Indiana

220. Name the Duke for players who are in the front office of an NBA team. (As of 2018).

Trajan Langdon is Asst. GM of the Brooklyn Nets

Danny Ferry is Special Advisor with New Orleans

221. Which former Duke player has won an NBA All-Star game MVP?

Kyrie Irving won the NBA All-Star MVP in 2014

222. Which two former NBA head coaches, broadcasters, and Hall of Famers were once Duke assistant coaches?

Chuck Dailey was an assistant coach at Duke from 1964-69

Hubie Brown was an assistant coach at Duke from 1969-72

A SPECIAL NOTE FROM THE PUBLISHER

I hope you enjoyed this Duke Trivia Challenge and that you enjoyed naming your own All-Time Favorite Teams. I enjoyed making the book. Although I took great efforts to ensure that my answers were accurate, it is still possible that I made mistakes along the way. If you find any glaring mistakes you can contact me at steve@dukebasketballdigest.com and let me know what editorial mistakes I need to correct.

I will from time to time (once every year or so) being making updates to the book. As Duke wins more championships and more players achieve certain milestones, the book will need to be updated.

Until then, feel free to follow my website, Dukebasketballdigest.com to keep up with your favorite team. And as always, GO DUKE!

Made in the USA
Lexington, KY
15 March 2019